Scriptures marked KJV are taken from the King James Version (KJV): KING JAMES VERSION, public domain

Definitions are taken from Merriam Webster online Dictionary www.merriam-webster.com

Entire contents otherwise Copyright @ 2018, by Tonya M Hutchings

Cover Design and Interior Formatting & Layout by **Quest Publications** (questpublications@outlook.com)

Copyeditor: G Renee'

THANK YOU!

Lord, I thank you first and foremost, for loving me and finding me worthy of your love. Thank you for coming to get me out of my mess. You are the reason this book exists. Thank you for encouraging me, pushing me, and seeing in me what I couldn't see in myself. I love you forever!

Taryn, Jordan, Jaiden and Joyner thank you for the encouragement and constant questions, "What chapter are you on now ma?" Also thanks for the total disregard for my closed door while I worked. The multitasking skills I acquired during this process have upped my game.

Mom, Erica, Dude, Mu and Tootie thanks for the pep talks, Face time calls and countless conversations during this writing process. I know you heard I'm almost done 1,000 times but you smiled and said "alright now!" each time.

To my SALT Community Worship Center family, you all are my greatest encouragers and biggest fans. Thank you for all of your support and encouragement. You are the reason that I believe God's love exists.

To all my friends, special friends and family that were with me through this whole process, I thank you. Your love and support was beyond anything I could imagine. There are too many to name, but you know who you are. I love you and I couldn't have done this without you saying every other day, "How's the book coming?" And I want to say from the bottom of my heart, LAY OFF GEESH! Lol

To my grandbabies –Amariah, Zion, Tripp, Elijah, Marley and Caiden thanks for understanding when Grandma had to say no. I love you.

To those who have hurt and offended me – I forgive you. And those whom I have hurt and offended – please forgive me.

And to you…for whom this book is written. This story has been a long time coming and so has yours. I pray that this helps you with the journey. Hold fast! Help is on the way.

I DID IT!

I DID IT! I FINISHED IT! I must say, writing this book has been one of the hardest things I've ever done. As I started this journey of reliving the painful memories of being molested as a child, I wasn't prepared for the inner struggles I would face. It is one thing to share your story one- on- one or even with a group in an intimate setting; But, to write a book about it that everyone would see (I mean, that is the goal right?), is a completely different ballgame.

The confidence and fearlessness I had in sharing my story of molestation so freely in conversation, took an unexpected nosedive when the medium went from word of mouth to pen and paper. I mean I had the same story, same passion but something changed in me as I began to SEE the words I had previously only voiced aloud. It seems backwards, that I would have hard time writing but be comfortable verbalizing my life experiences.

I learned so much about me on this journey. But, the biggest realization was that I am still growing, evolving, healing and maturing and that this process never ends! I've just learned to be more accepting of the process.

I asked myself, what is it that I want you to take away from this book. I had so many noble and lofty responses. I was really tripping! After I reread them, I realized they were not realistic!

So, here it is, I want you to cry with me, laugh with me, understand my struggles, but mostly, SEE me victorious! And if you find any of yourself in these pages, feel free to take with you what you can use. Well if you are ready, let's go but, hold on tight because it's going to be a heck of a ride.

TABLE OF CONTENTS

1. The Mirror Cracked 1
2. Perfectly Normal…NOT! 8
3. The Pursuit of Normal 11
4. Shame On You! 16
5. Bandages for Bullet Holes 23
6. Unforgivable—That's What You Are 30
7. It's Your Turn 46

1

THE MIRROR CRACKED

The summer of 1974 changed my life forever. It was the summer that I died.

The feel of hands, large, clammy hands around my ankles, snatching me out of dreams of fairytale princesses and knights in shining armor. His giant hands dragging me into an abyss. A darkness so black that its tentacles would reach far into my life for years to come.

"Please help me!" Those where the frightened cries of a defenseless little girl. Choking back silent sobs and screams, wishing someone would come and just STOP HIM! A scared little girl was looking for help that never came. Long days of dirty looks, probing fingers and violent threats gave way to endless nights of silent torment and torturous acts. It was the summer that I died.

The Appearance of Normal

Shame and guilt were my only friends. I was always fearful that someone would find the blood-tinged panties hidden in a toy box in the corner of the room. I limited my interaction with others for fear that someone would find out how dirty I was.

The only comfort I had was retreating to the fantasies in my head and playing with my favorite doll - Tiffany Taylor. She was the most beautiful doll I had ever seen. Okay, I know this sounds weird, but – her scalp swiveled around, and her hair would go from blonde to brunette instantly. She was a present from my parents, she was perfect, and I loved her.

It seems foolish now, but I remember the jingle from the 1970s commercial! It's funny the things your mind can retain! Yes, prepare yourself; I'm going to sing it, right here, right now!

Tiffany Taylor, (whistle)
She's what you want her to be,
First, a brunette turn- around she's a blonde - naturally!

Anyway, she was my safe place. I could spend hours pretending that Tiffany and I were doctors, lawyers and movie stars and we could jet-set all over the world, without me ever leaving the living room! She kept me grounded.

You are probably wondering, "Why is she rambling on about a doll?" It's important that you understand how important that little plastic doll was to my sanity. The constant physical torment to my body was one thing, but the destruction of my mind was something entirely different.

One muggy day, it was raining cats and dogs, and I went to the living room looking for Tiffany to calm my jangling nerves. I was always nervous when the house was quiet. I searched for Tiffany and could not find her. I began to panic as my search became fruitless. I went into my bedroom and fell onto the bed trying hard to hold back sobs. And then I saw it! Her foot was sticking out of the toy box like a flag pole. I desperately ran over to her, to hold her. I pulled her out, but to my horror, that monster had shaved her head bald. My mind snapped, and from that moment I was broken. He had taken the last thing that I had that was pure and beautiful and normal. My own image of self was completely marred, but Tiffany was perfect – perfectly normal to me.

I felt that there was no hope. Can you imagine a hopeless child? It's difficult to comprehend. Children are always hopeful!! They are always expecting something special or great to happen. But that day hope eluded me. Days and nights began to melt together and I was lost-adrift in a sea of darkness.

If you ever get the opportunity, you should research the human mind. It is absolutely amazing. It retains information and catalogs it in the most interesting ways. Stimuli are recorded by sound, scent, taste, sight and touch. And don't let me get started on how trauma is stored in a part of the brain called the amygdala. Another interesting fact is that this data is stored away until it is triggered by something familiar. For instance, the aroma of chicken frying may trigger a memory about grandma and visits to the farm (or the local chicken shack) depending on your upbringing.

My memories of this terrifying event were triggered by a song. I heard it so frequently that tortuous summer that it is permanently ingrained in my mind. I remember so vividly- that song- belting loudly over the radio as I sat in the tiny kitchen with my head leaned back against the wall. His sickening odor on my skin drowned out the delicious smells of greens, mac and cheese and fried chicken.

Little did I know that this would be the day the dam broke inside of me. The house was buzzing with excitement at the impending arrival of my grandfather and his new girlfriend. I was frightened and excited, and those warring emotions left my little body exhausted. The minute my grandfather arrived, the house was filled with laughter, dishes clanging and general merriment. But a tornado was brewing inside of me. I wanted so badly to just blurt out every horrible detail across the table, but terror and shame choked me like dry turkey.

As the evening came to a close, my grandfather and his friend began to stack plates high with food and wrap them to take on the ride home. I was a bundle of nerves. My body was trembling and my knees were incredibly weak. Everyone said their goodbyes and began loading bags into the car. Like a yo-yo being pulled by an invisible string, I paced back and forth in the kitchen. I had begun to panic. For some strange reason, I felt like this was my chance to get away from this horrendous monster and his torment. This was the day, and there was no turning back.

I watched as everyone came back inside the house for last minute goodbyes and I darted out the door. I had no plan. I didn't even know where I was going but I had to do something! And what did I decide to do? The only thing a panicked and frightened six-year-old child could do, I jumped right into the trunk of my grandfather's car.

There I sat…blinking…and waiting. My heart was pounding so loud in my ears that I felt dizzy. Then my grandfather's friend appeared from behind the car. She was startled to see me sitting there in the trunk amid all the bags. We exchanged confused glances and she, looking puzzled, asked me was I okay. All at once I felt the dam snap and every horrible detail of my summer poured out of me like lava. When I finally finished I sat there empty and hiccupping uncontrollably. She gently grabbed my hand and lifted me out of the trunk and said very simply, "Show me". That was it!

The next few days were a blur. Nothing was spoken of my confession. No one asked me any questions. It was as if I dreamed the entire conversation with my grandfather's girlfriend. I was stunned, confused and utterly broken. I just remember standing on the balcony in the hot sun retreating to one of the many fantasies in my mind.

I glanced to my right before going back in the balcony door and I stopped cold. My breath caught in my throat, and I was cemented to the spot. In utter disbelief, I moved closer to the railing. I couldn't believe my eyes. My parents were coming! My dad was running full speed toward the house. They were coming to save me! Before I knew it, I had bolted out the door, and ran down the steps, right into his arms. As I sit here writing this, I have no words for the emotions I felt that day! I had endured the worst summer any 6 year old could imagine, but it was over now. Daddy was here, and somebody was in big trouble. I was sure that the story had reached my parents by now. I mean, why else would they here so quickly?

As we prepared our things to return home, I waited for that monster to pay for all the sadistic things he had done to me and Tiffany Taylor. I waited for an apology as we got into the car heading home. As I stared out the window, I waited for those reassuring words that nothing like that would ever happen to me again. I waited… two years went by…then four and then six years rolled by and nothing was ever said about those horrible things that happened to me. I stopped waiting. It didn't matter any way. Tonya was dead, and no one even noticed.

2

PERFECTLY NORMAL... NOT!

Normal—Conform to a standard; average, typical, customary, common

—Mirriam Webster

I remember as a child, watching old shows about perfect families and desperately desiring to be like them. Tiffany Taylor had now been replaced by The Brady Bunch, The Jacksons, The Partridge Family and a host of other shows with seemingly perfect lives. They ate dinner together, worked out family difficulties, had family talks and even managed to have quality time before bed ("Goodnight John Boy", daddy would shout at the close of every show) and all done in 1 hour! They were perfectly normal families living perfectly normal lives in a perfectly normal world.

I longed for the lives that I saw on that small screen. I just wanted to be NORMAL! The wounds inflicted on my soul from that terrible summer were deep and bleeding profusely. I was spiritually and emotionally anemic, and I was lost. My identity had been stolen, and I had amnesia. Tonya was dirty, broken and empty.

But through those shows I could be whoever I wanted to be. I could be whoever others wanted me to be. I had become Tiffany Taylor. Do you remember those lyrics to the jingle in chapter one? If not, let me refresh your memory:

Tiffany Taylor, (whistle)
She's what you want her to be,
First, a brunette- turn around she's a blonde - naturally!

Now do you remember? Good. It's important to remember those lyrics for the rest of this journey. They are pivotal to understanding my thought processes during this time.

As I stated earlier, I was forever changed by that ill-fated summer. My formative years were riddled with instability. As a result of the trauma of being molested, I never wanted to see that family member again. It was easy because that side of the family was not close. It was easy to avoid him. I attended no family reunions, weddings or funerals. The sheer thought of seeing him would start nightmares and behavior problems no one understood. Shortly afterwards my parents divorced. The constant moving, frequent new schools, numerous identity and self-esteem issues compounded the train wreck inside of me. I was a mess. I felt worthless and insignificant. In my struggle to be accepted I began to mold myself into whatever I felt others wanted me to be. Like Tiffany Taylor, I could change my identity as quickly as you could change her hair color. I was a chameleon of sorts. If I needed to be good, I was good. If you wanted a bad girl, I could do that too! And as the years progressed, I was able to adapt to others desires of me – naturally. I was a plastic doll who could go from dark to light in an instant. Tonya no longer existed. I still had her face and even her voice, but her heart was empty and her identity lost. I lived in constant pursuit of normal.

3

THE PURSUIT OF NORMAL

Perception is a powerful lens through which to view our existence through. Essentially, every experience you have encountered, determines how you view life and others around you. Our perceptions determine our actions, words, thoughts, responses, relationships, need I go on? Perception is everything. It's the way we view or process information that is presented to us. It is also defined as one's insight or even wisdom. But it's all derived from the data we receive through experiences and what we are taught.

Why is understanding the concept of perception important you ask? A lot of my perceived views have had a negative or a positive impact on my mind, heart, actions and words. These perceptions shaped how I operated in relationships of all kinds. In many of these areas, I based

The Appearance of Normal

my interactions, responses and even made judgments of others based on previous encounters or experiences. All of us have done it. You don't believe me? How many times have you met someone new, and they reminded you of someone else? Based on prior experiences, you either judged them or felt an attraction to this new person. We measure new experiences based on our prior experiences. It's a learned behavior and a large part of the human experience.

In light of this, there are times when we judge someone or something without giving them the opportunity to prove or disprove our perceptions. I have missed out on some wonderful opportunities with some great people and situations simply because I judged them through the lens of some old data. But there have also been times when my perceptions were right on the money, and saved it me a load of drama and wasted time.

The definition of pursue is to follow or chase after something or someone. In my pursuit of normal, I found myself constantly comparing my life to others. I wanted a family, house, car, romance, acceptance, etc. just like everybody else. Remember that perception thing I was talking about earlier? Unfortunately, many times our perceptions are askew. I'm sure many of the people that I was comparing myself to, didn't have life any more together than I did. But, they looked happy and normal to me. I had no real basis to draw from. But I wanted to be considered normal just like them. I pursued it fiercely. Because I became a master at being what everyone wanted me to be, *appearing* normal came easy. But the black hole inside of me was consuming me from the inside out. I was shallow, lonely, empty, tired and utterly confused. I did not have self-worth or any concept of my own value.

This is very important! How you view yourself has a major impact on how others view you and how they interact with you. So the cycle began – I was devalued so I devalued myself. Because I devalued myself, others devalued me and so on. The more I pursued normalcy, the further away the view of my perfectly, amazing individuality became.

I didn't want to be different and unique. I wanted to be just like everyone else! Being me was painful and empty. Because my molestation was never addressed, I suffered with serious anger and resentment toward my family. On one hand, I wanted no part of them but on the other hand, deep in my heart, I wanted to be accepted and loved by them. Needless to say, I had issues.

I was Tiffany Taylor! I was a plastic shell with interchangeable identities and available to be played with by whomever possessed me at the time. I will spare you the details of all the stories of abuse, mistreatment, promiscuity, etc., that happened as a result of the

The Appearance of Normal

molestation. But I will say, it has been a long and difficult road. When your identity is not rooted and grounded in truth, (God's truth), you will be tossed by every wind that comes your way.

There were times when all I saw was darkness…all around me…inside of me. I carried so much shame, guilt and unforgiveness, and they were suffocating me…slowly. The terrible part was that the memories of the molester were still tormenting me. I carried his guilt and shame. This should have been his burden to bear. How had I become infected with it? One word- *unforgiveness* and it was my own concoction and it was like sweet poison. It tasted so good but it was killing me. If I had been infected with some type of a disease, perhaps I could have gotten medicine or treatment and received some healing. But my sickness was soul deep. There were no external scars or marks. Everything LOOKED NORMAL from the outside.

As we explore these next few chapters, we will look at these evil soul sicknesses individually. If you are still reading, and you find yourself identifying with me; my prayer is that you will take notes, meditate and devour the truth and light that God will share on how this terroristic trio employed by the enemy (shame and guilt, rejection and unforgiveness) tries to steal your identity and eventually your life. And you will learn how God defeats them and restores you!

As I look back over those years, I truly wonder how I made it through them. Although I had a limited knowledge of God, I now know that He truly kept me alive, if for no other reason but to tell this story in this season. If you have been in darkness, the lights are about to come on for you.

4

SHAME ON YOU!

Two of the main devices that the enemy uses to keep us captive and paralyzed in a mental, spiritual and emotional prison are *shame and guilt*! But how does this devastating duo operate? I reiterate that the enemy uses them to keep us captive or to paralyze us. That is exactly what they do. I want to take a little time to really dig in to the reality of guilt and shame. These powerful tools of the enemy kept me bound for many years in a mental and emotional prison that had me tied to my abuser with an invisible noose.

There are two viewpoints of guilt and shame that I want to discuss in this chapter so let's look at what Webster's Dictionary has to say about them. **Shame is defined as a painful feeling of humiliation and distress caused by the consciousness of wrong or foolish behavior; person, action or situation that brings a loss of respect or honor.** And **guilt is defined as the fact**

of having committed a specified or implied offense or crime. We can simplify these definitions by saying that shame's message says, "I am bad", while guilt's message says, "I did something bad".

Let me start by saying that shame and guilt are spirits. They are not human emotions. They are demonic spirits that are sent to make you feel rejected by God, others and/or to cause you to even reject yourself. I believe that my abuser carried much shame and guilt for his actions. I now understand what he was reflecting onto me; the torment that he was experiencing internally. The cyclical nature of these demonic spirits makes us want to pass our own guilt and shame along to those around us, so we blame them and/or shame them. So in essence, this dark, secret place in us multiplies in others.

There were so many times in my life where other people would admire something about me or tell me I was pretty, but I rejected those compliments. The spirits of shame and guilt would not allow me to believe that I was worth those inspiring words. I did not feel like I deserved the respect or honor of those around me. I always felt that if others knew what had happened to me, they would think that I did something to warrant it, or that something was wrong with me. I felt dirty and unworthy.

The guilt that my abuser felt, because of his actions toward me, created feelings of shame in him. His torment

The Appearance of Normal

caused me to feel shame, so I didn't tell anyone. The enemy tortured me with guilt by telling me things like, "you must like it", and "you want him to do this to you". This place of guilt and shame multiplied in me and I felt almost as much, if not more guilt and shame as he did.

These spirits kept me paralyzed in relationships with my family and others. I didn't trust anyone and the white hot anger was all consuming. The thing about demonic spirits is that there is no logic to their torment. I was angry at my abuser for his actions and threats. I was angry at myself for not fighting back or telling anyone. And I was angry with my family for not seeing what was happening to me, not protecting me and not vindicating me. The enemy had started a chain reaction in me that destroyed many relationships in my life. I entered into a number of abusive relationships and friendships and these spirits tormented me throughout.

The enemy's plan is to get you to focus so much on your past and the guilt associated with abuse or sin that you begin to see yourself as bad and unworthy of God's love or forgiveness. He wants you to be forever condemned to those negative experiences, influences, decisions and to never see the wonderful attributes and the healing that God has for you. He not only wants to make you miserable, but he desires to strip you of the one loving relationship you were born for. You were born to be in a loving and intimate relationship with God. So Satan's plan is to keep you so guilt and shame ridden that you don't feel worthy to approach God or even think of accepting Jesus in your heart.

That is the most devastating thing! Not only do you feel alone and unloved and you reject love from others and God, but you are unable to give genuine love as well. It's a lonely and fearful place. Always wondering if others know about your past or finding yourself pretending to be someone else to cover for your lost sense of self-worth. I remember feeling like a fraud most of my life. I wondered was I really a virgin? Will others know that I have been wounded so deeply? I always found myself trying to prove something to others and myself. All of the wonderful God given gifts, talents, ideas and dreams were being snuffed out under the dark cover of shame and guilt. But the unfailing love of God and the sacrifice of Christ saved me.

I remember sitting in my living room at the age of 36 tired and broken. I was trying desperately to figure out why I felt so empty and used up. At this time, I was a Christian. I was teaching bible study and singing on the Praise team, but I was so lost and empty. I was looking for answers in the word of God, and I came upon a passage of scripture that struck me. Ephesians 4:22-24 says:

The Appearance of Normal

[22] You were taught, with regard to your former way of life, to put off your old self, which is being corrupted by its deceitful desires; [23] to be made new in the attitude of your minds; [24] and to put on the new self, created to be like God in true righteousness and holiness.

For some reason, this scripture angered me. How did God expect me to just take off all the awful things that had happened to me and just put on this new person like nothing had ever happened? How was I supposed to forget my horrible past? Like my past was a shirt or coat I could just change like that? How could I have possibly deserved this? I shouted out into the empty room and asked God, "How can I ever do this?" I found myself depleted, shaking and crying while angry, hot tears poured from some abyss in my soul like a tainted fountain. This day started me on a journey to healing I will never forget. And it all started with an angry outburst to God.

Yes, I was a Christian at this time, but I began to learn that my relationship with God was in name only. I didn't know Him at all. My past abuse and bad decisions were tormenting me and condemning me to a life of pain and hopelessness with my saved and sanctified self. I gathered myself together and began to search the bible for some answers. I needed to hear God speak. I was desperate for healing. The shame and guilt were suffocating me and the fear of being found out was causing me to shrink from great opportunities. I searched the scriptures as if my life, or at least my sanity, depended on it. And then, as if the finger of God turned the pages, I came across the scripture that changed everything! Romans 8:1 said:

Therefore there is now no condemnation for those who are in Christ Jesus.

I was astonished! This one sentence cut through the fog in my mind, like a lighthouse beacon. I read it again. The words were like oxygen to a drowning person. My eyes were immediately drawn to one word. It stood out on the pages and began to seep into the jagged cracks and crevices of my broken soul. The word "now" resonated in my mind, bounced around my spirit and echoed through the chambers of my heart. Not only did it read that in Christ Jesus there is no condemnation, but it said "now" there is no condemnation. This moment, this day, this time, right now! The wonderful thing about the word now is that whenever those old fears and voices began to rise up, I had the assurance of that word NOW. It means there is no condemnation at that moment and 3 days later there is still no condemnation. If those things try to resurface five years down the road, "now" still applies. The voice of my accuser's guilt and shame were silenced for that moment. As I pondered over those words of freedom, I began to open my heart to the possibility that I could heal from that the terrible event. This one act, many years ago that started a chain of disasters in my life could be healed. I realized that shame and guilt were not mine to carry. They were not emotions or feelings I had to learn to deal with. They were demonic spirits. They were my accusers. And for once, they were silent. But a new battle had just begun.

> *And I heard a loud voice saying in heaven, Now is come salvation, and strength, and the kingdom of our God, and the power of his Christ: for the accuser of our brethren is cast down, which accused them before our God day and night.— Revelation 12:10*

5

BANDAGES FOR BULLET HOLES

Shame and guilt were formidable foes, but for the moment it appeared I was victorious. Life seemed to be cruising along a little smoother. I was married and heavily in ministry. The suffocating darkness was no longer as overwhelming, but I was still numb and empty. I could articulate the love and peace of God very well, but had never really experienced it. I had it down pat in theory but no idea what the weight of God's love felt like. I had marriage, ministry and family, everything I was so desperately searching for- or so I thought. But I was not prepared for the storm that was about to hit my outwardly normal existence.

The next culprit of that treacherous trio reared its ugly head and sent me and my life reeling: Rejection. Oh how I hate that word. So let's look at the root word.

The Appearance of Normal

To reject is to refuse to hear, receive, or admit: rebuff, repel. Rejection was the root that shame and guilt was anchored to. But where had it come from? In the light of molestation it would seem as if the victim is preferred by the abuser and not rejected.

The root of rejection is a very prevalent area to address in the lives of the abused, especially children. For me, I believe it began when I revealed the molestation. I was not heard. I was rebuffed. And my pain was ignored. The root of rejection took hold of my soul, and I felt like my life did not matter to anyone, not even God. That is one of the lies of the enemy concerning rejection. That foul spirit makes you believe its lies- that nobody wants or values you. You feel that you have no self- worth or worth to others. You believe the lie that not even God wants you. What a dirty lie! The truth of how fearfully and wonderfully made you are becomes hidden under the murky waters in your heart and mind.

Let's touch briefly on the root of rejection, and why it is so devastating to anyone in its grip. A root is the foundational structure of a tree. The health and vitality of the tree is greatly affected by the condition of the root. The root takes in the nutrients from the soil and rain, and it circulates the nutrients throughout the tree's structure. If the root receives nutrients from bad soil or a toxic water source, then the integrity of the tree is compromised. The leaves become frail and discolored, and the bark will be diseased and crumbling. The weight of the branches will eventually pull the tree to the ground. Just as a tree is anchored to the ground by the roots, the spirit of rejection anchors itself to the soul and heart of a person. It digs in deep and begins to draw its toxins and poisons from the enemy and his lies. He feeds you fears and doubts through the tendrils of those poisonous roots and begins to slowly destroy your self-worth, perceptions about love, and will even try to destroy your relationships with others and ultimately God.

Even in the midst of my marriage, I felt rejected and unloved. In a loving family I felt ostracized and unwanted. Oh, I played the part of the doting wife, mother, sister and friend. But on the inside, I never felt worthy of their love or acceptance. Perceived rejection of others gave way to self-rejection. I not only felt rejected by others but I rejected everything good about myself. I could not truly receive any compliments or encouraging words from others. That root was poisoning my entire system. My leaves were dying and the weight of the painful branches was pulling me to the ground. Once again I found myself spiraling out of control.

Oddly enough, in the midst of all this turmoil, pain and self-rejection, God was still reaching out to me. He was still showing His great, passionate love for me. His voice was still calling out to me through the darkness of my soul. He drew me to Himself through scripture. I developed a hunger for His word .I wanted to know all that He had to say about me. It's amazing the things that a person will do in search of answers. I was searching for God everywhere! But I neglected to simply just come to Him. I studied prayer and supplication. I studied worship and praise. I marveled at the most eloquent of intercessors and the powerful words that they bathed God in. I wanted to be like them. I wanted God to hear my beautiful exaltations and receive me.

Do you feel that way sometimes? Do you feel like you just aren't doing enough to show God how much you need Him or want Him? You want so desperately to feel His love and acceptance. It's almost like you are a spinning top and you have to keep moving because if you stop, you will fall. So there I was, bible study teacher, worship leader, teen ministry leader, and actively involved in outreach. I was teaching home bible study…you name it. God wasn't going to reject me because I was going to be the best Christian ever. I ran myself ragged, and yet I still felt no closer to God than before.

I want to take a quick side trip to talk about my marriage. There is a saying, "two broken legs can't run a race" (thanks son). And that's exactly what my marriage was—two broken people trying to run a race together.

He had a very painful past and so did I. We thought that when we got together it would be us against the world. But shortly after the wedding, the broken places began to show in both of us. Slowly, everything began to fall apart and the race we were running together became a race to see who would make it out alive. As I reflect back now, we were seeking something from each other that only God could give. That often happens with trauma survivors. They search for someone who can *fix* them or make them feel complete. It usually doesn't end well, and they both end up hurting. The children are wounded too. So, I found myself in the midst of a divorce. I was trying to adjust to raising kids on my own again.

One evening, after a very rough day, I broke down. I was mentally, emotionally, physically and spiritually drained. I lay in the middle of the living room floor unable to move. I had no strength and no more tears. I was completely depleted. As I lay there alone in the darkness, I prayed the most eloquent, impactful prayer I think I have ever uttered. I barely breathed out, "Daddy, Help! I am at the end. I have nothing else to give." That was it. There were no loud boisterous rousing prayers or unknown tongues. There were no scriptures or poignant quotes. Simply the quiet, heartfelt cries of brokenness.

I can feel the chills right now as I am writing this. In that dark place, He came for me. God spoke so loudly and

The Appearance of Normal

resounding in my spirit that I'm certain it was audible. He simply said, "Good, now I can take over." That was it! And at that moment, it was as if someone filled me with strength. He filled my body like helium rushing into a deflated balloon. The tears began to flow and I just knew that He was with me.

Days later, when I was reflecting back on that incident, I was led to a scripture that summed up that moment perfectly:

> *Whither shall I go from thy spirit? or whither shall I flee from thy presence?[8] If I ascend up into heaven, thou art there: if I make my bed in hell, behold, thou art there.[9] If I take the wings of the morning, and dwell in the uttermost parts of the sea;[10] Even there shall thy hand lead me, and thy right hand shall hold me.—Psalm 139:7-10*

No matter where I found myself, God would come for me. And even now, when I have hard times or those old thoughts of rejection try to creep in, I remind myself of those words.

The process of healing had begun. God was doing a work in me, and more importantly, I was letting Him. Was I delivered from the root of rejection immediately? No, but it was on the run! God's love had broken through the stony walls, and my heart was healing. I knew that it wasn't going to be easy, but I had no idea that the biggest piece to the puzzle was yet to be discovered. For now, I could survive with bandages over the bullet wounds. But soon those old wounds would start to bleed again and I would learn that in order to gain, I had to let go.

6

UNFORGIVABLE— THAT'S WHAT YOU ARE

Two down and one more to go! This fight would be the toughest yet! Shame and guilt were anchored to rejection, but unforgiveness was the gatekeeper. He was the one that held all the brokenness in place. His job was plain and simple, to keep me from forgiving so I wouldn't be forgiven.

That's it in a nutshell. And that's where you may find yourself right now. You may be angry, fearful and indignant. You may even feel justified in how you feel. Besides, you think you have the right to feel that way. Your abuser, molester, mom, dad, _____ (fill in the blank) changed your life forever. How dare they take away your childhood, dreams, safety, _____ (fill in the blank)? I mean that's how I felt. He ruined my whole life. I couldn't love, or trust or even have a genuine emotion. I was a plastic doll! I didn't ask for this to happen to me. I was a kid! The molester and his actions were unforgivable! Am I hitting home yet? I'll give you a second to pull yourself together.

That's where I found myself-stuck. My relationships were failing, I was having problems at work, I was physically ill and even my relationship with God was struggling. I knew the Bible says in Matthew 6:15:

But if you do not forgive others their trespasses, neither will your Father forgive your trespasses.

But God's amazing grace was sufficient for me. I was 36 years old when I finally found the courage to confront the molester. I was very angry and at a crossroad. I was tired of cycling in and out of darkness, and it was time to face my demons. But first, I had to confront my mother. All of my childhood was marred by the anger I harbored toward my parents because they had never addressed my assault. My father was deceased by this time, but my mother was still living, and it was time for a showdown!

I mustered up some courage and picked up the receiver. It was one of the hardest calls I've ever had to make. The words were like heavy stones in my mouth as she answered the phone. I mumbled out a quick greeting and some surface conversation as I gathered the nerve to ask her why she and my father had never addressed my molestation. Why did everyone act like it never happened? Why did they force me to suffer through it alone all those years? I was prepared to hear a variety of excuses and reasons why they had not talked about it at all. But nothing could prepare me for her response. She had no idea what I was talking about! She said that neither she nor my father had any knowledge at all of the molestation! She was completely dismayed as I shared with her what had happened to her baby girl all those years ago.

Now I was shocked and confused. There was a part of me that did not believe her. Why else would her and my dad show up to get us so quickly after I told my grandfather's girlfriend? She said that my grandfather called and told them to come and get us "A.S.A.P". but offered no other explanation. THEY WERE NEVER TOLD!! Now how was I supposed to process that? I reasoned that my grandfather decided that it was best not to tell my parents that their baby was being sexually assaulted. He made a choice that changed my whole life. I spent 30 years being angry at my parents for something they had no knowledge of at all.

I felt as if someone had dropped a house on me. I truly couldn't process this new information and now I had just dropped a bombshell on my mother. Needless to say she was hysterical and had a million questions-none of which

I could answer at the time. I had to find the pieces of my mind that had just been blown to smithereens. After my mother gathered herself, I told her that I would call her back so that we could finish the conversation. I had to get off of that phone. This new revelation was too much to bear.

Now I had questions that needed answers. Why did my grandfather not tell my parents? Why didn't I tell them? There were too many things going on in my head and I reached for the only lifeline I knew. I started to pray. The wonderful thing about God is that He knows all that you have been through good and bad. He also knows that there will be times that you have to confront those hard places. But in His wisdom and loving kindness He knows just what to say and do to help you get through it. And once again, He was right there to pick up the pieces. I cried out to Him in that dark place. I told Him about the feelings of betrayal, anger and confusion that I was wrestling with. I had spent 30 years mad at the molester, my parents and myself. Now I had to process these new feelings toward my grandfather. It was too much.

But, He is God. He knew this day was coming. He knew that I would need Him. He knew that I was ready even if I didn't know it. It was time for all those chains to come off. I had been bound so long that I didn't know I was a slave to my fears and to unforgiveness. I needed to be free. The Holy Spirit was so loving and kind to me as 30 years of grief, anger, shame, guilt and unforgiveness began to bubble to the surface. I was angry with everyone. He very quietly spoke to me that He would never leave me or forsake me. But from out of nowhere, those usually, soothing words caused a violent rant. Never leave or forsake me? You left a 6 year old baby…ALONE…with a sexual predator! Then you forsook me for 30 years!

Let me pause here and say that I DO NOT make it a regular practice to scream at God. I wasn't brought up that way. But I believe that God allowed this outburst to bring to the surface the real source of my anger. I was angry with GOD! It's still a little hard for me to say that. But the revelation of truth is the beginning of healing. Simply put, He is God right? He knows everything. Why did He allow such a terrible thing to happen to such a young child? He was right there! He could have stopped it at any time. He could have sent a bolt of lightning, or a black hole to swallow him up. He could have even sent an angel to deal with him. But, none of that happened. He did nothing-or so I thought.

As I sat there trying to process the guilt and fear of being angry with God, I began to feel this amazing peace. I can't quite describe it because it makes no sense. I was angrier than I had ever been in my life, but I felt so very calm. I could feel this tremendous love reaching out to me. I can only equate it to a tsunami. This love just overtook me and swallowed me up. Tears began to flow as the anger and intense emotions began to release. And there I sat, fully engulfed in His love. A love so pure and so consuming that it is impossible to describe.

It was then that the Holy Spirit began to speak. He addressed the unforgiveness I had against the molester, my parents, my grandfather, God and even myself. I forgot to mention that part. I harbored unforgiveness against myself as well. I did not know that I had unforgiveness against myself. I mean, I didn't do anything wrong. Did I do something to cause all these things to happen to me? But somewhere along the way, I had secretly begun blaming myself as well.

The Holy Spirit has a way of getting you to truly see yourself. It's not the face that others see, or even the one that you see in the mirror. He lets you see the face that *He* sees. He shows you your heart. I always felt that despite all the things that had happened in my life I was a loving and kind person. There is a scripture in Jeremiah 17:9 that reads:

> *The heart is deceitful above all things, and desperately wicked: who can know it?*

This was the most accurate scripture I've probably ever heard. Well, let me tell you, when I saw what was really in my heart, I was thrown for a loop. It was dark, and murky and full of anger. I had no idea that I had that much bile in my heart. Oh, I hid it well! I concealed it so well that I didn't even see it. This murky darkness was hidden under 30 years of swallowed pride, unfulfilled dreams, empty promises, and low self-image. There was a well of bitterness in my heart, and it was overflowing. The Holy Spirit lovingly walked me through each traumatic event of my life. He slowly unraveled the tendrils of darkness from my heart. He helped me to face my fears and my anger. Each moment I spent walking through traumatic memories was painful and almost unbearable at times. But I must say, He was with me every step.

Forgiving my parents was pretty easy. They had not done anything wrong. In actuality I needed to repent to them. I had put them through hell based on a "perceived" offense. I thought that they had neglected to help me heal from such a traumatic event. But in reality they were oblivious to the pain their baby was consumed in. A part of me is glad that my father was not alive to hear about the molestation. I think it would have been too hard for him to handle. My grandfather had been long gone. Although I didn't approve of his methods, I understood his logic. Even back then it wasn't really acceptable to talk about such things, especially in families. And besides, both of my parents were from some pretty rough neighborhoods, and my grandfather may have been afraid that my parents would've harmed him. But there was still one more thing to do. I needed to speak to the molester. He's the one who started all of this chaos.

I could feel the Holy Spirit with me in every step. I felt His leading as I repented to my mother and I made peace with how I had treated my dad. I felt God's love as I forgave my grandfather and released him from blame. But the task He was requiring of me now was more than I could take. I could hear the Holy Spirit's leading. He was calling me to forgive him. Forgive the abuser, the one who started all of this mess. Lord, you are asking way too much. Isn't this enough for today? I felt the old excuses and fears trying to take control. But the voice of God was louder and stronger in my spirit than I had ever heard. He was very clear that it was time to release these chains of unforgiveness in my life. I felt that the only one being bound was me. The abuser had lived his life and gone on to other things. I was the one in this prison of fear, rejection, shame, guilt and darkness. My unforgiveness of him kept me bound to him. So all my efforts to be rid of him and never see him again were fruitless. He was still tied to me!

Remember I said that I had stones in my mouth when I talked to my mother? Well, *Mt. Rushmore* was sitting on my tongue as I picked up the phone to call the molester. My breathing was erratic and my pulse racing.

The Appearance of Normal

But the Holy Spirit drew closer to me and His love for me started to break through the fear. He encouraged me that freedom was one phone call away. So, I made the call.

I won't bore you with the details of the call, but I will say it wasn't earth shattering or moving in any way. He didn't break down and beg for my forgiveness. As a matter of fact, he denied the whole thing. I was in shock! I just knew that because the Holy Spirit was leading me to call him that the Lord had already prepared him to apologize for all he had done. I just knew that the Holy Spirit would lead him in this conversation as God was leading me. But I learned that day that we are not all led by the Spirit of God - that's another book though. So, I just simply told him that I forgive him for molesting me and that I was releasing him from my heart and life. The words were so hollow in my ears; it was as if it wasn't me speaking. This was not the outcome I was expecting. No angels with harps or thunder claps. It was just me, sitting alone in a room with a phone in my hand. It was done! I had told him that all was forgiven. But clearly it wasn't that easy right? I didn't feel any different. I didn't feel this rush of love in my heart nor did I run outside and start dancing in the flowers. I just sat there blinking. Then, as if in slow motion, one tear began to roll down my face. Then another fell, and another and another until I could not control the tears anymore. I felt as if a baby elephant was trying to climb out of my belly through my mouth.

All the pain, grief, anger and resentment were coming out! And I couldn't stop it. All I could hear over the heart wrenching sobs was the Holy Spirit saying, "Yes, let it all go! Give it all to me!" And I literally cried until I could no longer keep my head up and I fell into the deepest sleep of my life. When I finally awoke later that night, I didn't know what was going on, but I definitely felt 100 lbs. lighter. I could breathe easier, and even my vision was clearer and brighter. Could all of that junk in my heart have caused so much noticeable heaviness and darkness? My answer is a profound YES! For the first time in 30 years there was no fog. If you are still with me, get ready to see some light.

Now, what is unforgiveness? According to Merriam Webster, unforgiveness is defined as "unwilling or unable to forgive". This definition implies that forgiveness is a choice, but you can also lack the ability to forgive. That's right, sometimes you may want to forgive, but you just simply lack the ability. The trauma has been so great and your life so devastated that you are paralyzed. You are stuck in that moment, unable to move forward and definitely unable or simply unwilling to forgive.

The enemy desires to keep you locked in unforgiveness so that you forfeit your blessings, your purpose, your future and your relationship with God. Unforgiveness is a dangerous snare that fools us into thinking that we have

The Appearance of Normal

a right to judge another or to hold a grudge for an offense or even a perceived offense. And that is exactly what we do; we judge them for their crimes and put them in a spiritual prison for life. But the sad part is, we get right in the cell with them! We rot in a spiritual jail chained to our abusers.

But God desires that we be free of all oppression and bondage. His desire for His children is that every hurtful event in our lives be healed by the power of His love. But how does all this forgiveness stuff work? I mean, you simply can't undo a traumatic event just like that. You can't unsee an act of violence or forget the blows of an attacker. So how do we forgive others? Is it possible to be in a place where you are not constantly tormented by your past? And God forbid if your abuser is someone you have to see regularly, then what? All of this seems almost impossible.

But with God, all things are possible! Forgiving someone who hurt you or someone you love is possible. First, forgiveness begins with a choice. What we must understand is that when we hold unforgiveness in our hearts against others, we have tried them in our own personal courtroom, judged them guilty and sentenced them to a lifetime of exile. That's essentially what unforgiveness looks like. We never allow them an opportunity to apologize or even try to make things right. We decide that what they have done to us is so horrible that they cannot be redeemed. So, every time we encounter them, we are reminded of what they have done to us and those old wounds start bleeding again.

Now believe me, by no means am I implying that being molested, beaten, mistreated, abandoned, rejected or any other traumatic event is no big deal. And do you know that people have even said to me," Get over it!" "That was 30 years ago!" I would have loved to have *just gotten over it*, but it wasn't that simple. It took work. Real Work! The Holy Spirit gave me a solid strategy that I will share with you. I will walk you through the steps of forgiveness as I walked through them. Here they are:

1. **Choose**
2. **Identify**
3. **Release**
4. **Heal**

1. CHOOSE

Forgiveness is not as simple as saying a prayer like, "Lord, I forgive so-and-so." Forgiveness is a serious decision to make. It's not easy and it can be uncomfortable or even painful, but the reward of going through it will be worth any pain you've experienced. Though we often see forgiveness as a challenging task, the reality is that the most important thing that we need to do is to choose to forgive. When there is willingness for a change to happen, then it is more likely to happen. If we are holding on to past hurts and unwilling to choose to forgive for any reason, then we will constantly find ourselves stuck in a cycle of darkness. Once you make the choice to forgive, the Holy Spirit will begin to empower you with His love and forgiveness. As humans, it is almost impossible for us to forgive in our own power. But by the power of the Holy Spirit we can not only choose to forgive, but we can walk in victory.

2. IDENTIFY

Identify the experience and express your feelings. Ask the Holy Spirit to help you label them as specifically as you can. Think back to what started these feelings. Who did this to you? When did it occur? Where did it happen? How did it make you feel? This step is very important. This is where the Holy Spirit leads you through various difficult scenarios in your life to help you identify the offense or the point of injury. You should know that your feelings will probably need time to catch up with your choice to forgive. Some days you will feel strong and other days you may fall to pieces, but just know that the power and leading of the Holy Spirit will be with you every step. God loves you, and He knows everything that is in your heart. Trust Him when He brings things to your remembrance. Sometimes we block out events from our past, but God knows even the number of hairs on your head. Also, please understand that your feelings are fickle. You can feel a million different ways about the same thing. You can love somebody one minute, and they can drive you nuts the next. Think about this: When you are listening to music, you can hear a song and be happy and joyful, and the very next song can make you sad or even lustful. But remember, your will gives you the capability to move beyond your feelings.

3. RELEASE

Once you have identified why you struggle to forgive and have a willingness to forgive, the next step is to let it go. As the Holy Spirit leads you to identify each person who hurt you, begin to release them from the offense. Call them by name and state aloud what they did to you. As you go through this process, allow the Holy Spirit to add anything you may have forgotten. Release them from the offense. Pardon them. Sometimes you may feel led to speak to someone in person, but it is not mandatory in this stage of the process. Let the Holy Spirit lead you in how to deal with people from your past. We can forgive others without allowing toxic people to undo all that the

Holy Spirit is working in us. Refusing to forgive provides a false sense of power, but this is deceptive, as it is really a cover for your own sense of hurt and vulnerability. Revenge feels good for a time; but, in the long run it does not work. The pain you give can never balance the pain you have received. So, refuse to be a victim. Forgive the debt. Move on with your life, and allow God to be the justice maker. Get out of the way and let God take care of it.

4. HEAL

Once we release it, we may find ourselves operating in a bit of anxiety. We may start experiencing thoughts like "What if this didn't work?" "How is this going to work?" or "I don't feel any different." These are fear-based thoughts generated by our ego and our desire to control things. Instead, trust and have faith in God that a change will happen. If you are in a place where you need to forgive someone or yourself, go through these steps as many times as needed; there is no limit. These steps are not meant to be a "do it once and snap everything changes scenario". It's something that we may need to do every day or a couple of times a day. You may need to try it for several days or even a week before you can begin to find yourself feeling lighter and freer. You should be dedicated to this process of forgiveness. When you are steadfast to the process, you will be able to truly forgive and have healthy relationships that reflect the love and forgiveness of God. Forgiveness is equally an event and a process. Forgiving an offender is an event. Finding release from your own pain and torment is a process. It takes time. It's important to keep opening your heart to God, be honest about your feelings and God's perfect love, mercy and grace will help you heal.

One day you will find yourself thinking differently about the one who hurt you. The intensity of your hurt will diminish, and you may even find yourself sharing your own journey from pain to forgiveness with others. One day you may find yourself praying for those who hurt you. Then you will realize you are free. Forgiveness is the gate to liberty. Think of the enormity of Christ's sacrifice and forgiveness of our sins. What a powerful display of love. Are you forgiven? Then you can forgive. God began by forgiving us; He calls us to forgive others. Your readiness to undertake the process of forgiveness is a show of how you appreciate being forgiven by God.

"To forgive is to set a prisoner free and discover that the prisoner was you."—Louis B. Smedes

7

IT'S YOUR TURN

For so many years I was tormented by shame, and guilt, rejection and unforgiveness. It would appear that I was progressing and then out of the shadows, those old demons would come for me. They would snatch me back into old insecurities and open old wounds. But each step in the deliverance process brought me closer to freedom. It didn't all come at once. I mean, it took me over 30 years to process into brokenness. So it is understandable that it takes time to process out into wholeness. But I want you to know that patience and self-love are very important while you are working it out.

I had to get to know the real Tonya. I had spent most of my life being deceived and in bondage to demons that had hijacked my emotions, mind and heart. They had imprisoned me: they stole my identity and my life. I had to learn to see myself the way God sees me and not through the eyes of my pain. I had to learn to love and have genuine affection for others. And I had to learn how to be loved. I had to learn that I was worthy to receive love. And you are worthy to love and be loved too.

In our lives we fight tooth and nail to be different. We want the newest shoes, flyest clothes, baddest house, nicest ride and so on. We want to stand out from the crowd and be unique. But we seem to ignore our own unique individuality when it comes to the things that matter most. We don't want anyone to know that we have been abused, hurt, mistreated or rejected. We look at the seemingly happy faces of others around us, and we desire to be just like them. You don't believe me? I'll prove it to you. When you look at the average social media sites, you see pictures of loving couples, families and friends who are smiling and enjoying life. We all want it and admire it. So we like the picture or even love it. But we don't always know the real truth about this family or couple. All is not what it seems. Maybe it's a picture of a loving couple celebrating their anniversary, sipping champagne as they stare into each other's eyes. But in reality they just had a horrible fight the night before, one of many fights. Or maybe you see the picture of a smiling family. But the picture doesn't show the heartbreak of the mother who is hurting because one of her children is on drugs. What about the husband's pain because his wife has been unfaithful?

The Appearance of Normal

On some level we all want to be perceived as normal. Maybe a person with a limp or a missing limb just desires to be seen as normal. But who sets the standard for normalcy? Why do we strive to be unique in some areas, but secretly desire to be normal in other areas? There is a very easy answer to these questions. We want to be in control. We all have flaws and insecurities - things we don't particularly like about ourselves. Things we can't easily change like height, looks, intelligence and body flaws. Things that make us seem different from others. These are the things that may cause others to bully us, isolate us or withdraw from us. It could be a lazy eye, stutter or even scars from an abusive relationship. No matter how much we as a people declare that we want to be unique and different, secretly we desire to belong. We desire to be a part of the pack. Why else would we have trends? The bottom line is this: We desire to be in control, especially of our own lives.

Abusers desire to control their victims. The abused feel that they have lost control in some aspect, so they seek control in other areas. Unforgiveness is a means of control. It says, I decide whether you deserve to be forgiven. But in the end, no one wins. My 30 year struggle with low self-esteem, anger, rejection, shame, guilt and unforgiveness started with one act of someone else exerting control over me. This one act sent me on a desperate search for control over my own life. You've seen this behavior before I'm sure. Someone who has been abused will use their body, money, power or any other means to be in positions of control. It's an ugly, vicious cycle.

But I have come to bring you hope! - yes you! I know you have been through a lot. You've been rejected and hurt. And maybe you feel vindicated in your anger. But I present this to you. All of the anger and resentment against those who hurt you is only designed to destroy you. That was the purpose in the beginning. Don't you see? You are destined for greatness!

You are made in the likeness and image of God. You are His creation, His son or daughter. Greatness is inside of you. God said that He knew you in your mother's womb. He had purpose and destiny all lined up for you. But from the moment you drew your first breath, God's enemy became your enemy too. Yes he was your enemy even when you were on his side. There is no good in him. And just because God loves you so much, he hates you. So, what does a bully do if he can't defeat the one he hates? He will try to mess with his family. But see, just like you will fight for your children when they are wronged, our Father in heaven fights for you!

He defeated your enemy! But because this enemy has already begun to attack you, he has likely caused some form of destruction in your life - like the pain of abuse or rejection. Like any wonderful father would, not only does

The Appearance of Normal

God deal with your enemy but he also heals the pain and removes the bondage. He gives you authority and power over your enemy so you can win.

So how does all of this tie together? It's pretty simple. Because you were destined for greatness, the enemy of our Father targeted you for destruction. He may have caused some really awful things to happen to you. You may have lost your way or even given up on life as a result. But because of the unfailing love of God, He comes today to offer you healing and deliverance from all the pain and bitterness. He wants you to see yourself the way He sees you:

"For I know the thoughts I think toward you, says the Lord, thoughts of peace and not of evil, to give you a future and a hope."—Jeremiah 29:11

Isn't that wonderful? He says He wants to give you peace and a future full of hope. You are His very own. He fashioned you in love, and for this reason alone will He fight for you.

When I started this book, I decided that I would not address the topic of "Why bad things happen to good people". I still won't. I don't fully know, nor do I understand why I was molested, why I chose abusive relationships or even abused myself. I have my theories. But, I do know this, of all the things I have been through,

I am stronger for it. For every horrible thing I have endured and survived, I learned that I was built to survive it. God gave me all that I would need from the beginning. And knowing this, I realize my strength.

I have learned many things on this journey. I started out a broken little girl seeking my identity from a plastic doll, television shows and other people. Now, I am strong, gifted, talented, compassionate, caring, loving, need I go on. All of those years searching to be normal like others, I have found how truly unique and amazing I am. Am I perfect—no. Am I growing...*YES*! Every day God shows me something wonderful and amazing about me.

All the lies of the enemy have been silenced and replaced with *truth*! I am loved! I am fearfully and wonderfully made! I work hard at keeping my heart clear of any unforgiveness. The enemy will come back every now and again to see if he can find me open to his old tricks. But as soon as I catch him, I remind him that he has already lost and I send him packing.

Now It's your turn to be free. Aren't you tired of being angry? Don't you want to just breathe? You can do it! God is waiting for you right now. He is with you right there, right now. He's waiting on you to say the words. Come on—I'll help you. Repeat after me:

The Appearance of Normal

Jesus, I believe that you are real. I believe that you are the son of God. I believe that you died and rose to save me. I need your help Lord. I've been hurting so long. I need to be free! Help me Lord to open my heart to you and allow you to heal me. I want to be free. I don't want to be angry or feel shame and guilt anymore. I don't want to feel rejected, and I want to be free of the chains of unforgiveness. I know that your word says that if I don't forgive, then you won't forgive me. I thank you for the grace and mercy you have shown me to get me to this place. Lord, I yield to your Spirit. Help me to be free. I am ready. In Jesus' name I pray Amen

Now, if you prayed that prayer with me, then get ready for God to take you on your own journey of healing and wholeness. You can do it. I'm rooting for you. And remember that God loves you, and so do I. Now go and find your own absolutely, awesome individuality in a world that is constantly in pursuit of normal.

Made in the USA
Columbia, SC
30 September 2019